I WAS THERE:

IT'S REAL

Inner Divinity Publication

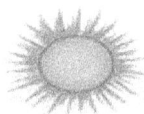

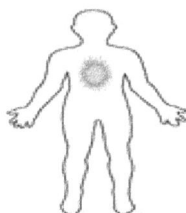

INNER DIVINITY

MINISTRY

I WAS THERE: IT'S REAL

By

Scott Campbell

2014 Copyright

By

Robert D. Campbell

Front cover By Andy Frasheski

Back cover by Anastasia Trekles

ISBN-978-1-312-35919-2

I would like to dedicate this book to those who have taken on the task and responsibility to seek out their own Divinity, for they are the ones who know their true identity.

And to those who have gone through the trauma of sexual abuse either as a child or adult, there is help out there for you. Please seek out the help and end the turmoil that is going on in your mind. If you can't find help, contact me.

CONTENTS

ACKNOWLEDGEMENTS

I must first and foremost give thanks to Joy and the happiness she has brought into my life and her immeasurable help with the production of this book.

To my sister Bernie, my church family David, Kevin, Sue and Jacque, and Sue S., I am extremely grateful for your kindness in taking the time and energy to edit and offer feedback on the manuscript. Your assistance and knowledge are greatly appreciated.

Dr. Lancer, thank you for being there for me. Your presence in my life has made a difference in so many ways.

INTROUCTION

Welcome to my story. I am glad to have the opportunity to share with you two life experiences that have shaped my path and changed my life. One involves a trauma when I was a young boy; the other an accident when I was a grown man.

But these events are where my story shifted. For it was a moment after my accident when I experienced what I believe to be a brief visit to Heaven, which inspired my emotional healing from the trauma, my physical healing from the accident, and a desire to search for a level of spiritual awareness that would pave my way to a closer relationship with God. I will start by telling you a little bit about myself.

I was born August 22, 1954 in Staten Island, New York City. My father was a career Navy man retiring after 23 years of service. My mother was a homemaker. I have three sisters, one older and two younger. I lived at home until after high school when I joined the Navy. When I returned home I held several jobs throughout my life, most of them in the food and beverage business. My last endeavor was with one of my younger sisters when she and I opened a gourmet delicatessen in High Springs, Florida.

Since my early childhood I have experienced underlying anger and fear which I have recently come to understand to be the result of being sexually abused when I was nine years old. Until my motorcycle accident in 2009, I had done an excellent job of burying the abuse somewhere deep inside, or at least I believed that was the case. But my behavior indicated these memories were not as deeply hidden as I believed. Everyday life would present triggers that would cause me to respond to other people or situations inappropriately, most often in anger. I didn't realize what I was doing or rather, what my anger was doing to me and to the people and things I cared about. I was unable to maintain healthy relationships and went through two divorces as a result. The relationship with my three daughters has not been as close as I would like. I now better understand the impact my behavior has had on others and how I once used anger as a disguise to express other feelings that I didn't want to acknowledge. Because

I kept my real feelings inside, I never really learned how to appropriately express feelings or how to feel comfortable talking about my feelings. They had always been something that remained unspoken. How do you talk about the pain you feel from guilt or shame or fear? And again, I wasn't even able to notice that I was doing anything wrong. I just thought I was having a run of bad luck or that everyone else was behaving badly. My insides were in turmoil but to me, that was what felt normal. But it wasn't normal, and it wasn't healthy, and it wasn't good.

So, I needed to begin exploring my true inner sense of self; thinking about the growth of my soul and the direction in which my soul was wanting me to follow. I knew I had an inner spark or flame that was waiting for the opportunity to guide me but it was being smothered by all of the toxins resulting from my guilt and other negative thoughts and feelings. I needed to do some internal housecleaning to find a sense of inner peace. Since my Heavenly experience (or what I also refer to as my time in the Light) I have received thoughts and messages from what I believe to be a divine source. They have changed my perspective on God, Heaven, and our souls. Where once I had a very conservative religious viewpoint, I now consider myself to have transformed my beliefs to a spiritual understanding resulting from a God of love who always forgives and wants us to do the same. It is through this understanding that I have come to learn to see others and myself in a more positive light and to realize the importance of forgiving.

My hope in writing this book is twofold. First, that it will bring comfort to and inspire those who believe in an afterlife to keep believing because it is true. It is even more magnificent than our human minds can explain or imagine. I know that many others have entered this other dimension and then returned. This book is meant to not only validate their stories and experiences but to find a way to process and share my own. For those not sure what to believe provide other possibilities or thoughts that might help them decide. My purpose is not to change the beliefs of you, the readers for you have the inherent right and the knowledge to seek the path that is right for you.

My second goal for this book is to support anyone who has experienced sexual abuse or any other type of severe trauma; let you know that you don't have to let the memories ruin your life. There is help out there. It can be a difficult road to travel, reliving those events all over again, but you can find the right support to guide you through it and little by little you can begin to let go of the pain you have been carrying for so long. You owe it to yourself to be free from mental turmoil, to be the best that you possibly can be, and to live the life you were meant to live. Can you even imagine letting go of the emotional toxins surrounding your trauma? I couldn't.

"We are not where our bodies are but where

Our souls are."

Donald Fisher

God Loves an Unmade Bed

THE ACCIDENT

I have heard it said that Heaven is just a breath away and I often have found comfort in that thought. Recently, I have come to believe that it doesn't need to be a breath away; it can actually be present in every breath we take and every thought we think. Why? Because Heaven is love. Love everywhere and within everything. The best example I can give of this is to imagine the one person or pet that you love more than anything else in this world and then raise that love to the 1000th degree. This is a beginning to the intensity and magnitude of the love that God feels for us and has provided for us. How do I know? Because of a motorcycle accident that broke me physically and then mended me emotionally. Three days before my 55th birthday, August 19th, 2009, at 10:05 PM, my life changed forever as I entered a two-month journey that would put me on a spiritual path unlike anything I had ever experienced. I was given a chance to experience time in Heaven and then return to my physical body.

The cool summer breeze blowing in my face that night gave me the refreshing feeling of endless freedom while at the same time causing a heightened connection to life. There was something about riding slowly on my motorcycle in the stillness of the night that was very peaceful and yet invigorating. I was riding my 1981 Gold Wing that I had rebuilt the engine on a couple weeks prior. After 40 years of accident-free motorcycle riding, I always prided myself as being a safe driver. I also realized I had no control over other drivers on the road and, therefore, could never be too careful. As I was enjoying all of the sensations of the ride and was approaching an intersection of two state roads, I noticed a truck with a couple of cars behind it stopped in the turning lane approaching from the opposite direction. I caught a glimpse of an elderly man standing outside of the truck with the driver's side door open. I slowed and kept my eye on him. His truck's left turn signal was blinking. I was just 100 feet from him and traveling at about 30 MPH. All of a sudden he got back into the truck and my heart stopped as I watched him pull directly into my path. I yelled "Nooo!" and watched as his headlight and his chrome bumper crashed into my left lower leg. I was immediately sent spinning like a helicopter face down looking at the road. I went 30 feet airborne. My bike was tossed 15 feet down the road. I remember thinking while flying through the air, "I'm going to land on my face." I was spread eagle spinning around and realized I needed to hold my head up and arch my back so I wouldn't land on my face. So I arched my back, threw my arms back so I would land on my chest, and then it happened – IMPACT!

All kinds of thoughts were going through my mind. I was still alive, still conscious, that was a good start. I wasn't feeling any pain and I thought that might not be a good sign. Was I paralyzed? Wait, I could move my right foot. I couldn't feel my left foot but I did feel a sensation in my left leg when I touched it with my hand. Great, I wasn't paralyzed. Then, when I tried to move, I felt a sharp pain as if I was being stabbed. I turned over onto my back and pulled my hands down to my sides. At the time, I did not realize how seriously hurt I was or the extent of my injuries. I was lucky that night as the man behind the pickup truck that hit me was a registered nurse. He came over immediately, held my head to keep my neck secure, continually talked to me; tried to keep me calm. I remember handing my phone to a woman who was there, asking her to call 911. She had already called and told me the ambulance was on the way. I thanked her gratefully. The RN did all he could do to keep me steady and secure. He kept asking me not to move. I sensed that he was very concerned about my condition and I began to get scared. Then my thoughts turned to my girlfriend, Joy, and how I wanted to see her again, perhaps just this one last time. I called her and told her what had happened, where I was, and asked her to come right away. Shortly after that I heard the sirens and could tell the ambulance was getting closer, and then I saw they had arrived. Time was a blur. In my mind it seemed I was lying there on the road forever but at the same time only a couple of seconds. I would later find out that it was five to ten minutes before the ambulance arrived. Our perception of time can be so distorted in certain situations and this was certainly one of those times. I did not know it then but while they were putting me in the ambulance, Joy had arrived on the scene. Unfortunately, I did not see her that evening or for the next 25 days.

Once the ambulance arrived and the EMTs came over to where I was laying, the RN who had stayed with me began telling them what injuries he thought I had incurred. I remember him saying "compound fractures," "broken ribs," and a "broken pelvis." I could not see any of my injuries so I had no idea what they were. One of the EMTs checked my blood pressure and pulse. At this point, my pain began to intensify and I screamed out as the pain came in surges. I felt a canvas around my waist; every movement became painful. They were shifting me onto the body board, tightening the buckles and straps and I remember yelling "You're killing me man!" Then they rolled me over to my left side, the side that had been hit. I felt stabbing pains again in my stomach; the canvas seemed to be holding me together. Even though I was in extreme pain, I noticed my lower extremities were starting to go numb. I was feeling pins and needles. I no longer felt the pain in my broken leg, but my broken ribs were making it hard for me to breathe. I could only take short breaths. As soon as I was in the ambulance the EMT started me on oxygen. I remember feeling like I could relax a bit now that I was getting medical care. The EMT seemed to be moving quickly and again I became concerned that I might be in real trouble. It seemed extremely bright as we sped away toward the trauma unit at Shands Hospital in Gainesville, FL. The next thing I remember is hearing the EMT talking over the radio to the doctor at the trauma unit. I heard him say "possible internal bleeding" then I heard the doctor say "insert a catheter." I started thinking "Oh no! More pain." I believe my pain reached its highest intensity as the catheter was being inserted. At that point, whether from the blood loss or because my body had reached an unbearable level of discomfort and fear, or for some other unknown reason, everything changed. I began feeling a gradual loss of consciousness; so slow, so easy and gentle, just a very peaceful feeling of letting go of my body and surrendering to the unknown, while welcoming a feeling of extreme love and well-being.

In what seemed like a split second, I was up in the right corner of the ambulance looking down. I could see the EMT and the head of a man and noticed that the man was me. Immediately, I was out of the ambulance and transcended to a different place. There was no tunnel, no light, no recognizable loved ones. Nothing visual. I heard

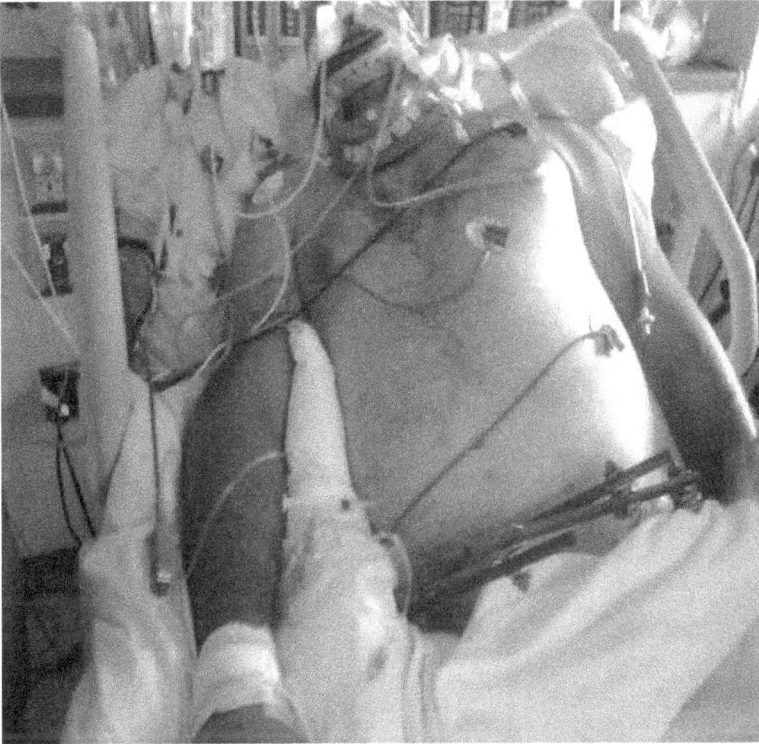

Three days after the accident my pelvis was put back together like a Jigsaw puzzle

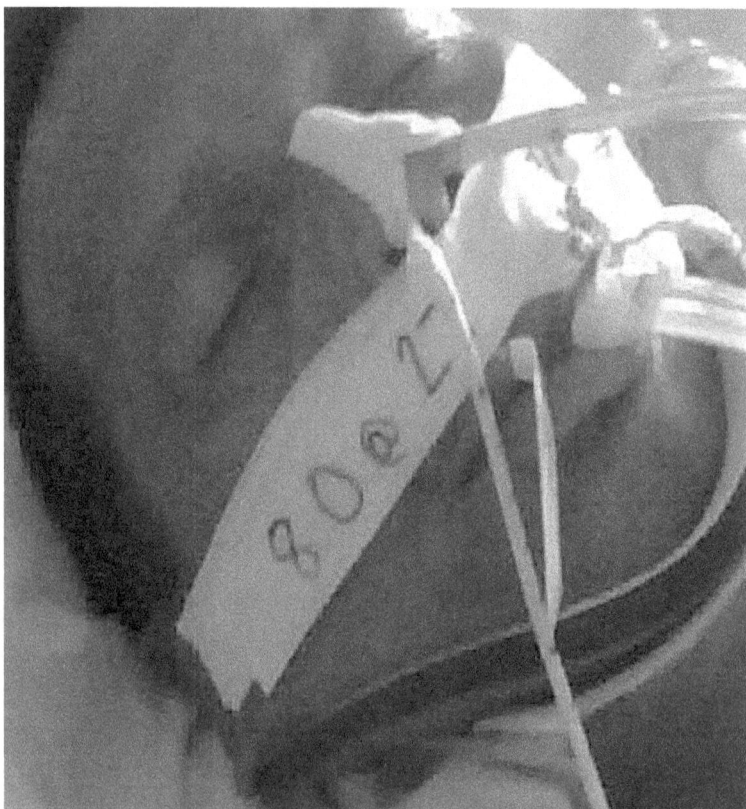

Three days after the accident

nothing and had no type of perception through any of my five usual senses. What I do remember was a rush of the strongest, purest love imaginable surrounding me and going through me in all directions, filling me and consuming every aspect of my being. It was as though I was dropped into a sea of love that erased any care or concern of my human existence. And at this point, I had no acknowledgement or memory of even having a human existence. Next, I sensed a being standing on my right, radiating this incredible love and light through a type of energy transference. The sensing I felt is difficult to describe but it is similar to when you feel someone watching you and then you multiply that feeling by 10,000. It was an inner knowing and understanding where there is perfect communication but not one word, one look, or one physical touch Is exchanged. In fact, there is nothing physical at all in this sensing. But this being made me feel so comfortable and I remember feeling like I was "home."

This being seemed to be the source of the extreme love I felt when I first transcended.

I know that this being and I spent time together and were at different places during this time. I have been unable to remember specific details about the places we were but I hope in the future I will be able to recall the places we visited. This being and I shared the feeling of love and light. My light was a rectangular energy that was completely enveloped by the brilliance of the light of the being. It felt as if we were one pure thought of joy, happiness, love, and light. As our time went on together the oneness with this being of light became stronger. Then I felt us go to another place, the last place we would be together. I began sensing other beings in front of us. I sensed these beings as oblong lights, individual beings of light but still somehow one, each a part of something greater. I wanted to be part of that something greater too. I didn't feel as connected to the other beings around me as I did with the being I spent all this time with. I didn't see or hear anything while all of this was going on; this is all something I sensed and felt. Then the beings of light that I sensed before and the being that had been with

16

me all this time started walking to what appeared as a wooden walkway similar to a boardwalk. One at a time they slowly approached a doorway. As each of them neared the door, before going through, each would turn and look at me. I felt a message but I have been unable to remember what the message was. Then, the being I had spent the most time with, the first one I had seen, was the last one and still with me and we were alone. I felt the being go to the opening, then pause to turn and look at me one more time before disappearing through the door. I wanted to follow them. I wanted to stay in this place that was indescribable pleasure and love. I approached the doorway and tried to go through the opening, but I couldn't. I said, "I can't open the door, my hands are tied." Frustrated, I was aware of a restriction and therefore was returning to the physical realm.

I would later find out that I had been in a coma for 25 days, and then had been in and out of consciousness for about a week. I really don't have any recollection of those last five or six days when I was in and out. I would respond to my family and the nurses and doctors but it is as though nothing stuck, except the feeling of being extremely thirsty.

The first vivid memory I have after waking up was feeling as though I was still immersed in the pure, unconditional, immense love. Then, in an instant, I realized I was back in my body and I felt the love that had consumed me vanish. To this day, I remember the discouragement I felt as it slowly seeped from me, as if someone had pulled a plug and it drained out and was gone. And in my mind I knew that I had experienced something that was not of this earth, and that I was going to miss that feeling, and think about it often. And like a dream or an experience that is too personal and precious to share because you fear that it would somehow be diminished by doing so, I kept it protected within my heart, safely guarded but yet available to me any time I needed to remember.

As my mind shifted to my surroundings, I recognized my environment as a hospital unit and I could remember the accident and the impact of the truck as it hit my left side. I saw that my leg was in traction so I figured I had a broken leg and no other injuries. I knew some time had passed since the accident occurred but had no idea of how long I had been hospitalized. Then, I noticed I had bars coming out of my pelvis and some type of plastic thing in my neck. I reached for my neck and the doctor came over and told me not to pull on the tube. It was there to protect the opening where the tracheostomy had been done when they needed to take the ventilation tube out of my mouth and enter through my trachea. He showed me how to block the hole with my thumb so I could talk. The first thing I asked him was if I could have a pair of crutches so I could go home and see my dog, Pickett. He said I was unable to walk so I asked him for a wheelchair. He then began telling me the extent of my injuries.

When I arrived at the trauma unit I had nine broken ribs, my left foot was completely crushed, every bone in that foot was broken and the foot was hanging on by skin and some tissue. There was a huge open wound on top of my left foot, my knee was turned to the inside, my hip was broken, I had two compound fractures in my lower left leg, and my pelvis was shattered. I was bleeding internally due to the bones in my pelvis severing four arteries, I was intubated (put on a ventilator) and sedated to an induced coma before leaving the trauma unit that night and going to the surgical intensive care unit (SICU). The primary concern the first night was the internal bleeding and the resulting fluctuation in blood pressure due to the bleeding. After 25 days in the SICU, I was moved to the 10th floor of the hospital, a general surgical ward. I stayed there for two days. I still had a feeding tube, a tube draining fluids from my abdomen, and a catheter. On the second day, I had a reaction to my medication and was very confused and hallucinating. The one thing I do remember from that day is that a friend of mine had visited and he was washing my face with a cool washcloth, wiping my lips and forehead and it felt so good. They were talking about transporting me to a rehabilitation center named Select later on that day.

Joy was with me through all of this and visited every day, staying as long as they would let her. Other friends and acquaintances began visiting too since I was out of the SICU. Since they would need to get me ready for transport, Joy went home and said she would meet me later at Select. I can remember calling her before they transported me and she was so happy because that was the first time I was able to call her since the accident.

I had so many people supporting me through the next months of my healing process. I left the hospital after gaining enough strength to lift myself up into a wheelchair and was able to transfer myself into the car. I got the external fixator, those metal bars that were holding together my pelvis, out on December 12th. That night I drove myself to my American Legion meeting where I had been a member for several years and currently was serving as Vice Commander. I had let it be known that I was going to be at the meeting that night. The Post Commander had put my initials on the Post's road sign the day after my accident, and left them up there until I came home to take them down myself. When I wheeled my way into the Post, it was full of Legionnaires and Legion Riders (motorcycle riders) welcoming me back to the Post. Some came as far as 100 miles to see me. I will never forget the camaraderie that night. Over the next five months, I got around by wheelchair and crutches. I got a titanium hip on April 10, 2010, and started physical therapy a week later. I then did rehab at the V.A. Hospital. I started out with pool therapy twice a week. After three months, I got my walking gait back. I then went to the weight room and started pumping iron!

I still hadn't mentioned to anyone about what happened while I was unconscious. For three-and-a-half years I kept it to myself, not even telling Joy. I love Joy very much, with every ounce of my heart, but I loved that being that was with me even more. I felt guilty; I felt like I had betrayed Joy or that I had cheated on her somehow because I wanted to be with the being of light more than I wanted to come back to a physical consciousness. I was disappointed when I couldn't make it through that door and follow those beings and live in eternal, unconditional, all-consuming and joyful love and light. The guilt was heavy. I know it shouldn't have been there in the first place but it was still there. My mind would tell me that there's nothing to feel guilty about but my heart still longed for that being; to be back in that realm or other dimension where I felt only pleasure, instead of being here in a body that was painful and no longer working the way I wanted it to work.

I soon came to believe and understand that the place I had visited was Heaven, and that Heaven is really our true home. In fact, it is Earth that we are visiting. I would hear spiritual people talk before about how Heaven was home, (many of the hymns we would sing in church indicated the same) and although I understood the message that was being given, I never before felt it in my heart, with every fiber of my being the way I do now. And the statement "we are not human beings having a spiritual experience, but spiritual beings having a human experience," completely resonates with me now. This was the first thought or type of message that would be constantly on my mind. I would meditate on this message and contemplate how it fit into my life, and it made good sense to me and felt right.

The first day that I was fully alert and aware after my accident I began getting pictures in my head. I don't know how to explain the way they came to me except to say they were extremely vivid and seemed so real. The first one was of me standing under a sphere of light and energy much like our sun. Then, a drop of the sphere separated and landed on me and I felt it spread throughout my entire body, beginning in my heart and then traveling to every cell of my being. I then became the same color as the sphere of light and I saw this vision off and on for the next couple of days. Then all of a sudden as I was experiencing this vision, the thought came to me that the ball of energy was God, and that the drop of energy that appeared to have landed on me was God's touch, and the light radiating through me was the energy of God. I felt the message that it was God's choice that I survived the accident and His touch that was healing me. This thought brought both a feeling of serenity and a sense that God cared very deeply for me. Over the next several days as I thought about this, it appeared to make sense, and felt right, but also seemed incomplete. I felt my thinking was on the right track but there was more to learn. I continued thinking about it, trying to grasp what felt like the missing link. Then I came to realize that the figure I saw and thought was me was in fact a representation of the entire human race, that God touches and heals everyone and that His love is in each and every one of us. And that made so much sense to me. I never really felt comfortable with the idea that humans were born in sin or that there was an opposing force we call Satan who was in a constant struggle with God for each of our souls. I knew that a God of love would love everyone equally and unconditionally.

Then one day, Joy and I were talking about the accident. The more we would talk, the more she would remember things that happened while I was asleep for those 25 days. I enjoyed hearing the details because it filled in the blanks in my mind and helped me to make the story complete. It's hard to lose 25 days and not know anything that happened during that time. She had kept a journal of the events and every once in a while she would pull it out and read some of the entries to me. I think this was healing for her too because she always enjoyed these discussions and several times we would end up laughing about some of the things that had happened, like the times when I was really confused. But on this particular day, we were really into the discussion and I said to her that I had something I wanted to tell her that I have been feeling really guilty about. Then I told her about my time in Heaven and how I wanted to stay there and not come back to Earth. She asked me if I thought the being of light was Jesus, but I really don't know. I can't remember any type of introduction or sensing of an identity. As a Christian I want to believe that it was Jesus with me, but all I know is that it was pure, unconditional love, a love that is indescribable. I felt brilliance, indescribable brilliance. Then she assured me that I had nothing to feel guilty about, that she could perfectly understand why I would choose that type of experience over an earthly one.

So, I had told the first person about my experience and it went well. Joy has had some metaphysical experiences of her own in the past and so she completely understood the significance of my experience and the impact it had on me. And, the best part was that I was able to relinquish my guilt and no longer felt that it was unfair to have wanted to stay in the presence of pure love. Slowly, one by one, I began to share my story with others, and it was always well received. In July of 2013, Joy and I had begun attending church at Unity of Gainesville and in August I decided to go in front of the congregation and tell them what I experienced. Again, the overall response was very positive. Church members told me about books written by others who had similar experiences and encouraged me to think about writing my own book. The teachings of Unity align very well with my experience of unconditional love and a God who loves us always, in all ways. In the years since the accident, I struggled with the question of why I had to return to my physical body and came to the conclusion that I still had work to do here, work that would involve helping others in some way. But first, I had to help myself. I began meditating on this and during my meditations, or contemplative time, I would receive messages or advice that helped me not only sort out some lingering issues I had, but also served as guidance on how to achieve the ability to accomplish one of the most meaningful lessons we can learn in this life: Forgiveness.

Me and Joy before one of our last rides.

JOY'S STORY

On August 10, 2009, I awoke to four big brown eyes staring at me, my Chihuahua, Teaspoon, and Yorkie, Maggie, letting me know it was time to get up and start our day. As I pulled them in to snuggle against me for just ten more minutes of quiet and stillness, the phone call I received the night before entered my mind and once again I felt a shiver run through me and couldn't help wondering what happened to the caller. Who was he? Why was he so upset? How did his voice find its way to my telephone line? Without caller ID on my phone, I couldn't even tell if the call was local. My "hello" was met with the sounds of a man in severe pain or anguish, moaning, crying, and unable to form words.

"Who is this?" I asked. More moaning.

"Are you OK? Are you OK?"

Silence.

For the next couple of days that call would cross my mind several times, and each time a feeling of concern would accompany the memory. Why did it still bother me? Was he reaching out to me for help? I tried to rationalize that it could have been a crank call or someone who realized he had the wrong number, but a subtle feeling that came from within me knew that there was more to it than had appeared at the time. To this day, almost five years later, I remember that call vividly. Not because of the communication that lasted less than 45 seconds but because that same exact call would occur less than two weeks later. This time, the caller would be identified and the purpose of the call would lead to a two-month journey that would not only be one of the most devastating events of my life but would take the caller through a physical experience of hell, and then a spiritual experience of Heaven.

Scott and I had been dating less than two years. We both were in our fifties and had been previously married and divorced. We met at the local American Legion shortly before my ex-husband and I separated. My ex and I would stop in there for a drink now and then, and Scott was the vice-commander so occasionally we would see each other and just say a few words. When Scott heard I was separated, and at this point I knew the separation was final, we began talking and getting to know each other. Then one Sunday he called me and said he was going to a

Christmas party and didn't want to show up alone and asked if I would I go with him. He said I didn't have to answer him then but could give it some thought. Over the next week, we began talking more and I felt pretty comfortable with him and thought it might be fun to go on a date, even though he said it would not be a date, but we've all heard that before, right? Besides, I have to admit that when he told me he had his third- degree black belt in Tae Kwon Do I thought that was pretty sexy and that it might be fun wrestling with him. I also admired how dedicated he was to veteran affairs and that he was himself a Vietnam era veteran. My Uncle Gary was killed in Vietnam so I had a tender spot in my heart for those who advocated on the behalf of soldiers and veterans.

We decided that before we went to the Christmas party we would go out for dinner and maybe dancing afterward. When I asked him if he had any trouble finding my home, he said "No, because I drove by a few days ago to make sure I knew where it was so I wouldn't be late for our first date." Now tell me, how endearing is that?

While we had several things in common such as a passion for pets and animals of all kinds, love of nature, and similar spiritual beliefs, we also were very different. In many ways, Scott was free-spirited and enjoyed doing things that I thought were "risky," particularly riding a motorcycle. While I viewed riding as the potential for pain and broken bones he saw it more as wind in your hair and a feeling of freedom. Okay, so one of us was going to have to give a little. However, I also realized that I wanted to lighten up a bit and start doing some things that I had never done before; so by the time spring came I had a helmet, chaps, riding boots, and all of the other accessories. We would spend Sunday afternoons going different places on his bike and I did get to the point where I enjoyed riding.

It was late afternoon on a Wednesday, August 19, and Scott and I had been discussing some of our views on religion and spirituality, as well as some of the books we had recently read on the topics. While neither of us would consider ourselves religious in the traditional sense, we both feel a very strong presence of God in our lives and continually strive toward a higher level of spiritual awareness. As the afternoon was giving way to early evening, we thought it would be fun to get out and take a ride on his motorcycle. I had wanted to get my hair cut and since Scott had nothing else to do we decided that this would give us a chance to get out and enjoy some fresh air while also getting something accomplished. I called the salon I usually went to but they were closing in twenty minutes. I called my second choice and was told there were no openings this afternoon. Another call to a third salon and I was told again, no openings. Finally, I called a fourth salon and was told they could do a haircut in one hour so I made an appointment. Since it would only take about twenty minutes to get there, we had some time to just hang out at home. After about ten minutes, the clerk from that salon called back and said she had made a mistake and there was no opening this afternoon. When I hung up, I made the comment to Scott that "it almost seems like we weren't supposed to go anywhere tonight." So, we decided to spend the evening at my place. At around 9:45 PM, Scott decided he would go home. I walked him outside as always and he told me he would call me when he got home. He pulled to the end of the driveway and got off of his bike to close and lock the gate. I remember looking back and seeing him and thinking, "He doesn't have on his helmet; I wish he would wear it more often." I went back inside and decided to spend the rest of the evening reading. After about 15 minutes, my phone rang and I remember thinking it was too soon for him to be home. I answered my phone and there it was again, the moaning and sounds of extreme pain. My first thought was "Oh no, it's the same exact call from a couple of weeks ago." Then, after a couple of seconds, I heard, "Baby, I wrecked my bike. Someone t-boned me."

"Did you call 911?"

"I don't know if anyone did, I'm on 235, can you come?"

"I'll call 911 and then be on my way."

All of a sudden, I felt frozen and yet knew I had to move fast. The person at 911 told me that someone had already called about that accident and an ambulance was on its way. Then the thoughts came into my head:

"Why didn't I ask him if he was okay? Wait, he called me so that means something; at least he probably doesn't have a brain injury. Why didn't I tell him I love him? I wasn't thinking." So many thoughts were going through my mind.

Before I was out of my driveway, a woman called on my cell phone and said she was with Scott and he wanted to know if I was coming. I told her I would be there in about 10 minutes. A few minutes after disconnecting with her, I was at the point on the highway where I thought his accident had occurred and he wasn't there. I had the wrong road in mind but I knew his route home so I would eventually find him. I decided to call his sister and let her know what happened so I pushed her contact number, held my phone to my ear, and the woman from before was on the line.

"How much longer will you be?" she asked.

"A few more minutes. Is he OK?"

"I don't know, I think he has a broken pelvis."

"I'll be there soon."

I disconnected again and tried a second time to call Scott's sister. I touched her number, held the phone to my ear, and again, the woman from the accident site.

"The ambulance is here."

"OK. I'm almost there."

Finally, in the distance, I saw the red lights from the emergency vehicles and police car.

"Thank God!"

I remember my anxiety level being so high that I was functioning on automatic pilot. As I pulled off to the side of the road I could see the motorcycle still lying in the middle of the street. It looked bad and there were parts scattered around it. A policeman approached my car and asked who I was.

"The man on the motorcycle is my boyfriend. Can I see him?"

"No, I'm sorry but they are just putting him in the ambulance."

"Please, he called me and asked me to come."

"They are working on him and will be leaving in a couple of seconds. Meet them at Shands trauma unit."

I left the scene and headed for the ER. A couple of minutes later the ambulance passed me so I knew at least he was on his way. I dialed his sister again and got through and explained what had happened and she agreed to meet me at the ER.

I would later find out that the reason Scott wanted me there and was so concerned about me getting there before the ambulance was because he didn't think he was going to live and wanted to see me one more time. One of the things I could never make sense of was how the woman who called remained on my phone and even after I dialed Scott's sister her voice came through. I would be silent waiting for his sister to answer and yet somehow she knew I was on the line and would start talking. That

36

was the third strange event that happened that evening. First, not finding a salon which kept us from getting on the bike together, then the strange phone call that began exactly like the one a couple of weeks before, and now this woman who was on my phone even after breaking the connection and dialing another number.

That evening as I sat in the ER waiting to hear how he was doing, I felt like he was going to be alright because of the phone call he had made to me. And, at that time I thought, even if he had a broken pelvis that couldn't be all that serious. Little did I know! When the doctor from the ER came out to talk with us (by this time Scott's sister had arrived), we were told that they were having trouble stabilizing his blood pressure due to severe internal bleeding. Apparently, bone fragments from his pelvis had severed four or five vessels and they could not get the bleeding under control. Also, he had broken several ribs, had compound open fractures to his left lower leg, and his left foot was basically hanging on by the skin. At this point, they were giving him blood transfusions and had intubated him so his lungs wouldn't have to work so hard. They also sedated him to the point of an induced coma. We were directed to the surgical intensive care unit to wait for more information. Soon after we entered the waiting area, a resident came in and explained that his primary concern at this point was the internal bleeding; so as soon as Scott was stable enough to undergo the procedure they would be cauterizing the vessels that were bleeding. I later found out that they had given him 23 pints of blood that first night and that the trauma folks were squeezing the bags so the blood would go in faster as dripping the blood in would have taken too much time. At around 3:00 AM, he was taken to the procedure and afterward I went home to get some rest.

I returned to the hospital at around 6:30 AM on Thursday, the following morning, and was able to see Scott for the first time around 8:00 AM. Prior to entering the SICU, I was told of the tubes he would have, that his body was significantly swollen, and that he would be unresponsive due to the sedation. By this time, I was so overwhelmed and unable to take in the vast amount of information I was given and by necessity, or survival, my brain had put me into a state of emotional numbness. I heard what was being said and could repeat it but did not seem to be able to have access to or express the emotions that were overwhelming me on the inside. I remember thinking late in the day how horrible it would be if the phone call I got from Scott after his accident was the last time I heard his voice and the memory of the sound of his anguish and pain would be his final farewell to me. It also struck me how strange it was that his voice was the same as the call from a couple of weeks before, in fact, exactly the same. I could not make sense of it and at the time there were so many other things that had priority that I could only think of it as something unexplainable. I never have figured out that phone call and I think about it often. I am familiar with metaphysics and believe that a divine source intervened to keep me off of the bike that night. I also can make sense of the woman on the phone as a type of intervention helping me to stay in contact with someone on the scene and also to assure Scott that I was coming to him. But that phone call, to me, makes no sense and in no way was helpful. Perhaps it was a premonition manifesting in physical form, or an event that just occurred out of sequence, if that sort of thing even happens.

By Friday morning, Scott was stabilized enough to undergo surgery on his left ankle and foot. He had seven pins put in that foot and they fused his ankle bones together. They also cleaned out a huge open wound on the top behind his toes that extended back to his ankle. The area of his fractures needed a skin graft but that would be done at a later date. The surgeon put an external fixator on his pelvis to hold it together which he would keep on for about three months.

Over the next several days, I really didn't know if Scott would pull through this or not. I would stay at the hospital with him from 11:00 AM until 10:00 PM, holding his hand, rubbing his head, and doing everything I could to send him positive, healing energy. I would talk to him and tell him what was going on and every day I would repeat everything that happened to him. His nurses said that it would be helpful to do this and I believed at some point, even if he didn't understand what I was saying, he would find the sound of my voice comforting. The things that I remember the most during these days was when he would open his eyes, which he did for the most part only when he was being turned over, there was such a blank expression on his face, like he was looking into outer space. It was as if he was not inside himself. It was also very painful to hold his hand and squeeze it, or gently kiss his lips and get nothing in response. I functioned in an internal state of panic; always expecting the worst to happen but trying to maintain faith that God would see us through.

For the next couple of weeks things were up and down every day. Since visiting hours began at 11:00 AM, I would get there around 10:50 AM. There was a phone outside of the SICU and in order to get into the unit you had to call the desk, say who you were and who you were there to see. Along with other families there to visit loved ones in the SICU, I often was waiting in the hall by the phone a couple of minutes before 11:00. I always dreaded calling the desk because almost every morning they would tell me Scott was having something done, but they could not elaborate, so I naturally would think that something had gone drastically wrong. Many mornings something had deteriorated significantly and they were attempting to stabilize him. I can remember thinking everyday how much easier it would be to just turn around and run then to make that call because of the fear and apprehension that seemed so overwhelming. Many of the others waiting to get in to see their loved ones experienced the same feelings and this was something we often talked about; perhaps it helped knowing each of us was not alone in what we were experiencing.

On August 29, Scott's youngest sister, Liz, came down from New York and spent the week with me. We spent the majority of our time at Scott's side, watching the monitor that was reading out all of his vital signs and keeping an eye on him. Scott has three nurses in his family so we had to take pictures of all the tubes that were coming out of him, so they could see for themselves. They also wanted to be updated on any new procedures. We were able somehow to find some humor in our paranoia and figured the nurses on the unit considered us a real pain. However, they were very good about answering our questions and doing their best to make us feel comfortable. I gained a new respect for nurses, their knowledge, and their roles in helping their patients during this time. At some point during this week they replaced the tube going through Scott's mouth into his lungs with a tracheostomy.

Scott continued having problems with his blood pressure, lung volumes, pneumonia, kidneys, heart rate, concerns about blood clots, and many other issues that would come and go. As time went by, I was becoming less positive about what the outcome might be. I spent many hours thinking about our short relationship but how I felt like I had known him for so long. Many of our times together would cross my mind. Like a couple of weeks after we started dating and we had gone to a veteran's service for Veteran's Day. Scott had to stay there and help take down the tent when the service was over, so we drove separately. When I was leaving, traffic was backed up so far and I thought I would never get out onto the main road. He said, "I will take care of that," and he walked out onto the main road, stopped traffic, and let me out. He certainly earned points for that one.

Back to the SICU - when Scott's lung volumes were stable enough, he was taken off of the meds that were keeping him asleep but he didn't seem to be waking up. I remember thinking "what if he just keeps sleeping forever?" Not one person up to this point had told me that he was expected to live, so I didn't know what to think. As it was about three weeks after his accident and no real change or stabilization noticeable to me, I was feeling exceptionally discouraged and was crying when one of his doctors saw me in the hallway outside of his door and asked me what was wrong. I told him that I was concerned about Scott's prognosis. He assured me that they were all very pleased with his progress and there was no reason to believe he wouldn't make it through this and get back to a very normal life. He also took the time to answer all of the questions I had and this made a world of difference in my overall anxiety and fear about the situation. Shortly after this conversation, one of Scott's residents also explained things to me and told me it was normal for people not to wake up for several days after being taken off of sedation.

On September 12, Scott woke up from his coma. He was very confused but did remember being in the accident. He could not talk because he still had the tracheostomy tube and could not write because his hands were still so severely swollen he couldn't get his fingers to hold a pen. After a couple of days they did something to his tracheostomy tube and showed him how to hold his finger over the hole in order to talk. He remained in the SICU until September 21 when he was moved to a general ward on the 10th floor of the hospital.

On September 23, shortly after being given his medications, Scott became very confused. He saw rats climbing the wall and believed that there was someone sleeping under his bed. He grabbed ahold of each side of the external fixator (the metal bars used to hold his pelvis together) and began shaking it saying, "I almost have it." We would later wonder if this was at all related to him trying to get through the doorway in Heaven. When his student nurse came in to ask a question, Scott's reply was, "We're all high on drugs." Most likely a pretty good explanation of how he felt. He also did not know where he was or what type of a building he was in; thinking it was a schoolroom rather than a hospital room. Overall Scott was doing so much better that the doctors decided to move him to a rehab facility later that day. I decided to get out of the hospital for a while and go home and meet Scott at the facility later that afternoon. While at home, my phone rang and I answered it. On the other end of the line was Scott saying that the helicopter pilot was in his room ready to take him to the rehab center. Since he was being moved only about a mile from the hospital, I realized he was still confused so I asked if I could speak to the "pilot." His doctor got on the phone saying that the person he was referring to was the ambulance driver who would be transporting Scott. As I hung up the phone, I was overcome by a feeling of hope because that was the first call I had received from him since his accident and even though he was still confused, his voice sounded so wonderful.

I met Scott at the rehab facility early that evening and by then he was thinking more clearly. Finally it seemed like things were in a constant state of improving and he was going to be OK. Slowly, over the next couple of weeks, the tubes came out and his body started healing; doing its job without assistance. On October 20, 2009, Scott came home. He still had a long way to go with his rehabilitation and healing as he'd eventually have an artificial hip on his left side as well as a couple of minor surgeries. However, he did far better than anyone expected. He was so determined to heal and did everything within his power to get his body back to functioning the way it should. I was so proud of him for how hard he worked. A couple of days after he went to the rehabilitation center he told me about his out of body experience in the ambulance when he looked down, saw his body and the EMT working on him. At that point, that was all he said he experienced. It would be close to three-and-a-half years later before he shared his time in Heaven with me.

One of the most difficult things for me to release and let go of was my general feeling of the fragility of life and the fear that something else terrible was going to happen to Scott. I know that in many ways I was overprotective of him after having seen him so close to death and being by his side for several weeks not knowing if he would survive. This was frustrating for him and I could understand that. I tried my best to let him proceed as he felt able but it was extremely difficult. I was so worried about his every move and fearful that he was going to be reinjured. The first time he tried to walk, the first time he drove, and other accomplishments that were major milestones for him caused me extreme anxiety. At the same time, I was so proud of him for all of the hard work he put into his recovery and how well he did, that eventually I learned to take a step back and trust his judgment and instinct on what and how much he should do to get to the best physical condition possible.

There also was an emotional recovery. Soon after I returned to work on my usual schedule, I remember coming home one day finding Scott very upset and crying. He had lost so much at that point: his health, his work with veterans, his independence, he was in extreme pain, and certainly had every reason to feel depressed. He was able to stay alone at that point but not to drive, so he was isolated during the day with only time to think. And, because each trauma we experience has a tendency to make us revisit other traumas in our lives, negative events from his past also began surfacing. My heart ached so badly for him and I wished there was more that I could do. I now understand that some of his depression no doubt resulted from his memory of being in paradise totally free from any physical limitations felt on this earth, and his reality of returning to a broken body with no idea of why he was still here.

THE INCIDENT IN THE WOODS

When Joy and I began considering the idea of attending a church, it took us quite some time to really commit to the idea. After all, prior religious experiences had left us both with more questions and, in the end, feeling more separated from religion than when we began, but most of all not feeling very good about ourselves or our relationship with God. It seemed to us, at least from our personal experiences, that some of the basic premises of traditional religions were so very different from what we felt in our hearts. Although the two of us have some minor differences in our views of spirituality, we think very much alike on the overall picture. To clarify, when I say *spirituality* I am referring to each of our personal relationships with our Creator and creation and the ways in which we manifest that relationship in our lives and envision how it will be when we leave this earth.

My accident and the experiences afterward had left me with a need to feel closer to God and to learn more about the magnificence of our Creator. After all, I believed I had been in the presence of God for a short time and I wanted to learn how to carry that feeling through to my life on this earth. I wanted to find some structure in this exploration and again my thoughts turned toward attending a church. We had heard some really good things about Unity of Gainesville and how it was different from many other churches and so decided to give it a try. We both left the first service feeling very positive and uplifted. Finally, a church that focused on God's love for us and aligned with our belief that God is everywhere, in everything and everyone, and therefore always around us offering love all of the time.

Wait. If God is everywhere and in everyone, what about those people in my life who I felt had hurt or betrayed me? Am I supposed to love them as if those things never happened? How can I forgive much less feel love for someone who caused me so much emotional pain that led to me making some pretty lousy choices in my life and distrusting people in general? I still carried a lot of anger toward those people. And what about that one incident that took place in the woods? Could I really learn to think about that young man in a way that didn't haunt me and leave me feeling anxious and demoralized? I could tell that if I was going to connect with my Creator in a way I never had before, I was going to have to face some really difficult challenges.   If I was serious about welcoming God's love into my heart and shining it onto others, I had some tough emotional work ahead of me.

When I was in kindergarten my family had moved to Kittery, Maine, to base housing for my father's last duty station at Portsmouth, New Hampshire, Naval Station. During the year we lived in Maine, my father was helping contractors build a home for us in Hopewell Junction, New York, and I traveled back and forth with him for that year. During that winter, it was my job to collect wood for the fireplace, our only source of heat during construction of the home, so I felt like I was helping out by supplying the wood. On these trips, we would stay overnight in a very old tavern from the 1800's called the Hopewell Inn and my father became very good friends with the owner. I felt like this was a special time for me and my dad to share and even though I was quite young at the time I still remember those trips fondly.

In 1961, my father retired from the Navy and relocated our family to the home he had helped build. The house was complete on the outside but still needed work such as the inner walls, hardwood floors, closets, and a few other finishing touches. My father got a job working for IBM during the week then delivered mail for the post office on Saturdays. My mother was a housewife and did most all of the work around our home and yard. Since my father worked so much of the time, Mom was the one who spent the most time with us and really raised us. I had one older sister and two younger sisters, and I have always thought of my family as close and caring. I can remember when we moved to our new home we all were so excited. The road we lived on was in the shape of a horseshoe and was one mile long. Our house was at the top of the hill and the closest homes were two houses a half mile below us. In one house lived a boy my age, Donny, and we became best friends. Next to him lived an older boy, Benny, who was about five years older than Donny and me. The space between those two houses and ours was all woods. My greatest pleasure at that time was exploring the woods with my German Shepard, Duchess, learning about all of the wonderful sights and sounds that nature had to offer. My parents allowed me some freedom to roam around in the woods as long as I let them know where I was going.

Those woods were pretty deep and one time I did get lost and Duchess stayed right there beside me. I was calling out for someone to hear me and finally my call was returned by my mom, so Duchess and I followed the direction of her voice and found our way home. The next time I was lost in the woods did not turn out to have a positive ending.

At the end of our road was a creek called Fishkill Creek. It made a sharp bend right at the corner of the intersection of our road and Beekman Road. I liked going down there to fish and would often go alone. It was in the fall of 1963 when I was nine years old, and I was down at the creek just hanging out skipping stones. Benny, the older boy who lived next door to my best friend Donny came walking down to where I was standing. I noticed he had a rifle in his hand. I asked him what he was up to and he said he was going to go check some of his traps and asked if I wanted to come along. At that age, I was interested in trapping (though I never had tried it before) so I was thrilled to be asked along and I followed him. We strolled along the creek for a long time and then turned left away from the creek and headed deeper into the woods through some dense trees and foliage. I was trying to remember where we were going because I had never been this deep into the woods before. I began trying to make landmarks in case I ever came back again but soon gave up because everything looked so strange. Benny was walking in front of me carrying his rifle in his right hand. I was excited about the idea of checking the traps and what we might find. Then we came to a field and there was a stone wall that we followed for a while. I had never been in this area; never had seen this field before. I really didn't know where I was. We walked along the edge of the field and walked into the woods at the other end. We walked about another twenty minutes into the woods. I really had no idea where we were but everything seemed to be alright. Then all of a sudden Benny laid his rifle against a tree and started to urinate. I thought it was strange that he didn't turn around, away from me. He stood facing me so that I could see his penis. Next, he pulled out a cigarette and put it in his mouth and lit it with his penis still hanging out of his pants. I remember thinking how big it looked. Other than my own, it was the only one I had ever seen. Then he walked over to me with it still hanging out of his pants and said, "You know, when guys get older they start doing things for their friends. You're my friend, right?" I didn't say anything because I was in shock from him standing there in front of me with his penis hanging out. Then he said, "I want to put my dick in your mouth." At this point, I knew something was drastically wrong.

"I'm not going to let you do that. It's disgusting." I said.

He walked closer to me and asked me again and said, "There's nothing wrong with it." He put his right hand on my left shoulder and pushed me down to my knees and again said, "I want to put my dick in your mouth."

"No! It's disgusting."

I tried to get up and he pushed me back down on my knees and began slapping me on my face. Fear came over me instantly. I had never been hit like that before, by anyone.

"Let me put my dick in your mouth."

"No!" And I clamped my mouth shut.

He began slapping me again only harder this time. He began getting angry and punched me in my chest right over my heart and then continued hitting me in the face. Now, it was more like punching. I tried to get up and he pushed me down again and held me down by putting his left hand on my shoulder. Then he grabbed his penis (I noticed this time that he had an erection) and he began pushing it into my mouth putting his hand on the back of my head to steady me so he could get it in. I turned my face away and shook my head back and forth to tell him NO, as I did not want to unclamp my lips. I was extremely scared at this point. I didn't know what he would do next. I was still on my knees and he began slapping me harder, pushed me back again and I fell on the ground. My fear was escalating and I began crying. He reached down, grabbed me by the arm, and pulled me back to my knees. He put his left hand behind my neck again, held his penis with his right hand, and shoved it into my mouth. I gave up and didn't fight back anymore. I was so scared that all I could think about was going home. I just wanted it to be over. I kept saying to myself, "Just do what he wants and you can go home." I kept repeating that to myself. So I stopped fighting and gave up, letting him push his penis into my mouth. I didn't resist anymore. Then he told me to move my tongue around and he pushed it harder into my mouth. His penis hit the back of my throat. I will never forget the taste, the saltiness from him just urinating. I gagged and felt like I was going to throw up. I jerked my head back, and he said to me, "Let's try it again" and he pushed it back into my mouth. He told me to move my tongue around and he kept telling me I wasn't doing it right. I must have frustrated him because he pulled it out of my mouth, stepped back, and started to masturbate in front of me. I had no idea what he was doing at the time. I started crying; I was scared. I kept seeing the rifle out the corner of my eye, leaning up against a tree. I didn't know what he was going to do. I thought of grabbing the gun like I had seen on TV westerns but I didn't; I was too scared to move. I just waited, still on my knees sitting back on my feet crying, hoping he would not try again. Then he pulled his pants back up. To this day, I can still see him standing there with the cigarette hanging out the side of his mouth, under his upper lip, looking like a real greasy punk, masturbating. He grabbed his rifle and started walking back the way we came. He didn't say anything; he just started walking. I didn't know how to act or what to do.

I didn't know where I was, so I started walking back with him, staying about 15 feet behind him. I was afraid of him now. I had never been slapped or punched in the face by anyone to this point in my life. My sense of safety had been shattered. The world, and especially those woods, would no longer be a carefree, exciting place to explore. I had just been introduced to the sad realization that there were some pretty awful things that could happen, even when you think you know the person you are with.

As we walked back, nothing was said. It was a good 45 maybe 60 minute walk. I was scared the whole time and I didn't know what to expect next. Would he stop and try again? Would he do something else? We finally got to the creek so I knew where I was and felt a little better. We walked along the creek until we got to Beekman Road. Then we got to the part where we go up the embankment to head back home. Just before we started going up the embankment, Benny turned around and looked at me, with his gun in his hand shaking it saying, "Don't you tell anybody what **we** did today. Otherwise I'll come and get you." I never said anything for 47 years. The way he said "What **WE** did," made it sound like the act was mutual and would lead me to feeling guilty for many years to come. It would be over 45 years before I realized that "*WE*" did not do *anything*. It was not a mutual act but was a fifteen year old sexually abusing a nine year old.

Benny took a lot from me that day. I no longer felt like an innocent nine year old. My view of the world became one of mistrust of others and always being on guard. Because of the inner struggle I was having with the guilt of thinking it was partly my fault, I began building a wall around myself and knew that I would do anything possible to keep a similar situation from ever occurring to me again. It also made me a very angry person, and as a teenager I was always standing up for my friends or other people who I felt needed defending. I could not stand the thought of someone being taken advantage of or manipulated by another person, particularly if it was someone I cared about. I was out to get the bullies. I began thinking of ways to assure that I would always be able to defend myself and others.

When I was fifteen I got interested in martial arts and began taking Tae Kwon Do classes. I did very well and worked my way up to a third-degree black belt and became a member of the Mooduk Kwon, a Korean martial arts honor society. I competed throughout the state of North Carolina and even throughout the country, as well as two fights in Helsinki, Finland, at the World Cup Championships. I had a 27-3 professional record in the ring. I think every time I got into the ring to fight, I was subconsciously fighting Benny. The feeling of hitting someone felt good. I liked to hear the grunts and groans of my opponents when I would connect with a solid shot that I knew hurt them. It would drive me harder; it was like a rush of adrenalin. Then I would hit on them harder till either they didn't get back up, they conceded or the referee would stop the fight. I came to realize that I enjoyed hurting them. When I would see them crumble I would have the feeling of victory. Later in life I would realize that it wasn't victory I was feeling, it was vengeance. I hated Benny for what he had done to me. I wanted other people to feel the pain I was carrying. I wanted them to feel what it was like to get hit hard, to feel defenseless. Subconsciously, I guess I felt that I couldn't tell anyone about what happened to me but I sure as hell could make them feel some of the pain I felt. However, as so often is the case, especially with trauma and abuse, the physical pain heals but leaves behind a much stronger emotional pain that lays inside of us and lingers, simmering, until it reaches a boiling point. Being in the ring was my way of releasing my pressure from that boiling point. I now regret that my success in martial arts was a result of my anger and need for vengeance but I didn't realize this until years later. My emotional pain masked itself in a hundred disguises that I never recognized or even knew existed. I was really fighting the incident in the woods and all of the fallout resulting from carrying around guilt because I was unable to defend that nine year old boy back in Hopewell Junction, New York.

A few years after the incident in the woods I heard that Benny got his draft notice. Some of his friends took him down to the induction center at Whitehall Street in New York City. Benny failed his physical examination and he and his friends were celebrating this by drinking beer on their way back. While they were driving home they got into a car accident, and Benny broke his neck. He wound up being paralyzed from the neck down. He was 18 years old and he got full military benefits because he was coming back from his induction physical.

I saw Benny once after his accident. His parents were trying to get him out of their car and they were putting him into a wheelchair. I could see his limp arms just flopping around. His legs were just hanging there. I watched as they tried to jerk him into the wheelchair. I often thought about the accident that paralyzed him. At first, I thought that it was God's punishment to him for what he had done to me and what he made me do. Then my feelings about his accident shifted and I started thinking that God let that happen to him so that he would never be able to hurt anybody else. For many years, that was what I believed. Now, I give Benny full accountability. Just like I was not at fault for what Benny did to me, God is not accountable for Benny's paralysis. God has given us the gift of free will and Benny used his free will to take advantage of me, and to drink and drive.

My desire to stand up for others manifested in a more positive way during the late 1980's. In the early 1970's, Montag nard refugees who had fought with the Americans in Vietnam began resettling in Raleigh, Greensboro, and Charlotte, North Carolina. They came to the United States as political refugees. For twelve years after the U.S. had left Southeast Asia, the Montag nards continued to fight the North Vietnamese. Whole villages were trained by Green Berets to defend themselves against the North.

Lutheran Family Services became the organization that coordinated the resettling of the Montag nard refugees. One of the groups already in North Carolina had to leave two hundred of their members in Vietnam when they came here in the 1970's but those members would soon be arriving. One of the social workers at Lutheran Family Services introduced me to one of the tribal leaders of the first groups who came here. I got to know him and members of his group quite well. He later asked me to help resettle the new group that would be arriving in the near future and Lutheran Family services offered me a one-year contract to help the new refugees adjust to the United States. Some of the members of the new group had never been out of the jungle.

My job was to coordinate healthcare services, help them acclimate to their new environment, help them find jobs, and make them self-sufficient in one year. This group consisted of all ages, from infants to senior citizens, and about equal numbers of men and women. It was amazing to me that all of the teenagers and adults had bullet wounds. These people had been through so much and had the scars to prove it. They were very hard workers and were so appreciative. Every one of them who was of working age found employment that first year and all of the children were attending school. I was so concerned that after I left someone would take advantage of them because they were such a polite and well-mannered group of people. One time, I was taking a group of four to the Health Clinic and we had to get on an elevator to go to the floor where they were going to be seen. They had never seen an elevator and were reluctant to get in. When the elevator doors closed and the elevator started up, they all had a look of fear on their faces. I gestured "It's OK." When the door opened they looked out, walked over to the window that was in front of us, looked down at the ground, and then all turned around with big smiles on their faces, shaking their heads "YES" and gesturing to me that now they understood.

After my year was over, I did a two-year follow up and they were doing very well. It was so good to see them again and to have them share with me how far they had come in their efforts to resettle. They seemed well adjusted and were doing fine on their jobs. Some had even found better jobs by this time. It was such a privilege and an honor to work with them and to be a part of their lives in a manner that I thought really made a difference. To this day, it is the highlight of my life and it helped me learn to focus on life outside of myself. We were working for the benefit and survival of the group. I have many cherished memories from that year.

Moving forward, in 2010, several months after my motorcycle accident, I was coping with the pain and life changes I had recently endured and I was still getting angry over things that were really no big deal. If someone would say something I didn't like I would let them know. After my competing days, I never hit anyone but I would raise my voice and get up in their faces and would really respond inappropriately. People were starting to see that I had anger issues. The consequences of my anger turned many people against me and impacted my ability to be successful in many situations. Joy and I talked about the possibility of me seeing a counselor or psychologist. Although my anger was never directed at Joy, she had been with me at times and saw how I responded to others when I got upset. She began to get concerned that I was losing all of the things I cared about because other people were tired of dealing with my attitude. I'm sure it also was embarrassing for her when she was with me and I got angry at someone. So I made an appointment at the Veteran's Administration Hospital in Gainesville, Florida. I began seeing a psychologist, Dr. Lancer, for therapy. During our first session we were talking about my anger and how I was getting mad all of the time and I didn't know why. I didn't say anything about the incident in the woods until I was getting ready to leave that session and I finally said to him, "I probably need to let you know that I was sexually abused at the age of nine by a 15-year-old boy." He sat straight up in his chair and his eyes opened up wide and he said, "We have to deal with this first." At that point, he highly suspected that my anger was a result of the abuse and told me about a type of therapy called *Prolonged Exposure* and how effective it was at helping people who had experienced trauma or abuse. The therapy would consist of my telling him over and over again what I remembered about the incident in the woods and it would be recorded each time for me to take home and review between sessions. I said I would do anything that might help me learn to control my anger. We scheduled an appointment the following week for a PTSD assessment test.

I showed up the following week. I tried to tell him the story but I couldn't. I was crying so hard; completely overcome by my emotions. I don't remember ever crying as hard as that day in his office. Aside from the crying I did while Benny was hurting me, this was the first time I cried about the incident. The pain was just pouring out of me and Dr. Lancer was so patient. He didn't say anything or try to get me to stop crying, he simply allowed me the space to release what had been buried inside of me for so long.

I came back the following week and was able to share the experience as I remembered it from beginning to end. I was crying again but was able to keep sharing my story. It was on the third or fourth visit when the session was recorded and I took the recording home to start listening to my explanation of what happened. While listening, little by little I would recall bits and pieces of events that I had forgotten took place back in those woods. Each week after that we would record our session and I would take that new version home and listen to it, and again, it would spark other things that happened and more details. I had noticed the more I listened to it, the clearer it became. I got to the point where I could tell the story without crying. I finally realized that the incident in the woods was not my fault. For years I had blamed myself. I thought that maybe I didn't fight hard enough. Maybe I should have just turned and ran away. But I didn't think of those things while the abuse was happening. All I could think about was I wanted to be at home. An incident like that is something you never forget and it changes you. I am so grateful for having the opportunity to work with Dr. Lancer and all of the help he gave me in working through my feelings. The type of therapy he did allowed me to collect all the bits and pieces of that incident that had been scattered through my brain and file them all in one place. The program that Dr. Lancer worked with me on was not easy. At first, it broke me down completely. But I feel I had to be broken down so I could start over again and rebuild myself, my emotions, and my thought patterns in stronger, healthier ways. I now have tools that can help me if I fall back into negative patterns. When I finally got to tell the complete account of the incident in the woods, a tremendous weight was lifted off of me. I physically felt that baggage leave me. I still can remember the feeling that I had while driving home the day I completed telling the experience. It got easier as time went by. I kept working on the assignments and listening to the recordings, and all of the work paid off. It will always be there in the back of my mind. I'll never forget what happened that day in the woods, but now when something reminds me of it, although I still think about it a little, I don't get angry at myself. I am satisfied with the way I handled the situation that day. There was a gun at the scene and I'll never know if Benny would have used it if I had made him mad enough or didn't go along with what he wanted. There were no traps that needed to be checked so he had the rifle for a reason. The way I now see it, the bottom line is that I got to walk home, be back with my family that day, and have been able to live my life. Many children never make it home once they become a victim of sexual abuse.

"Show mercy, that you may be shown mercy; forgive that it may be forgiven you. As you do, so it will be done to you; as you give, so it will be given to you; as you judge, so you will be judged; as you show kindness, so will kindness be shown to you; the amount you dispense will be the amount you receive."

I Clement

FORGIVENESS

Through therapy I came to understand that I had nothing to forgive myself for and I was then able to release the guilt I carried for so long. I learned how to not judge my actions that day and understood that I did what a nine-year-old boy should have done to survive. I did, however, still need to learn how to show kindness to myself, and even gratitude that I was able to walk out of those woods and back to my home. Even though I was able to let go of my guilt, I still held on to many negative patterns of thinking and behaving that, by now, had become so deeply ingrained that they seemed almost instinctual.

One evening in 2012, when I was driving home, I realized I did not remember driving the distance I had and then I began feeling very strange physically. I even wondered if I was having a stroke. My head was pounding. I pulled off of the road because I didn't know what was happening. Then, I heard a voice say to me, "You MUST forgive Benny." I thought, "What? Where is that coming from? Forgive Benny?" I hadn't even been thinking about Benny. So I sat there and thought about it for a few minutes. What a realization. I had forgiven myself but never thought I could even begin to forgive the person who had made such a negative impact on my life. How would I begin? I didn't know if I could do that or not but the one thing that I now understood is that I had to try. Then I realized I felt fine, the pounding in my head and weird physical feelings had stopped, so I drove the rest of the way home with no further incident.

But how would I go about forgiving Benny? Did I even want to? It was time to put everything I had learned to work. So I thought, and I read, and I asked questions, and I meditated; and then I thought more, asked more questions, and meditated more. I had to take a long hard look at what I had come to believe since my accident and apply those beliefs to how I felt about Benny.

So what had I learned so far? I know from my experience in the Light that there is such an indescribable, powerful love when we are able to shed our earthly bodies and our egos and be in the presence of God. I believe that a few people have learned to feel this love here on Earth, like Jesus and the Buddha, Mother Teresa, and a few others but by far the majority are searching for it or do not even realize it exists. I know that I have not been able to get the feeling back since I returned to my body, although the memory remains very strong and vivid. And, I have come to know that the feeling of pure unconditional love is something unlike anything I have ever known or even imagined.

Attending Unity church really has helped me to understand some of the many thoughts that were going through my head and to make sense of some of the Bible scriptures that no longer appeared to align with the beliefs I now had about God. I felt even stronger than ever about God being all around us, loving each of us, and forgiving us for the mistakes we make on this earth. Unity teaches us that God is everywhere and that there is a spark of God in each of us. Hmmm. Did that mean there was also a spark of God in Benny? Well, I guess it did. But this really brought up a huge question in my mind which was, "Why, if there is a spark of God in all of us, do some of us behave so ungodlike?" And that is where I believe free will steps in. My understanding led me to the conclusion that we do each have that spark but we don't all choose to see or acknowledge it in ourselves or in others, and we let our egos overshadow the light. That is why some people can hurt and torment others or do things that some would say are behaviors brought about by "Satan." History has provided us with many examples of egotistical behaviors: Judging others, wanting more, wanting what someone else has, thinking others are not equal to oneself, hating others, and the list goes on and on. And what about low self-esteem or not loving yourself? The belief that we are not as good as others has led many people to choose some of the worst behaviors imaginable. They have been told by others that they are not worthy and they chose to believe the opinions of others. But who could feel they weren't exactly who and what they were meant to be if they felt the love of God within them and knew that God is always a part of them and surrounding them all of the time?

So, I let go of my childhood belief that there was a devil constantly tempting us trying to entice us into giving our souls to him instead of to God, and in doing that I came to the realization that it was not an evil force inside of Benny that made him hurt other people but rather, his inability to feel the God within him, or, his choice to listen to his ego instead of acknowledging his God within. I began to view sin as separation from God. The more I thought about this, the more I noticed that my opinion of Benny was changing. He was no longer appearing to me as a monster that I hated because of what he did to me. I could now think of him as a human being who most likely had some pretty bad things happen to him in his life, possibly even sexual abuse. But even if he was never a victim of such actions and his male hormones were just taking over his body, he chose to act them out on someone else. I no longer took his actions as a personal attack on me and who I was but realized that I was in the wrong place at the wrong time. I had to walk past Benny's house that day in order to get down to the creek, and he most likely saw me walk by and knew that I was alone. So to him I seemed like an easy target.

Four years after my motorcycle accident, in 2013, I had an opportunity to go back to Hopewell Junction where I grew up. While I was there I went looking for the grave site of Donny, the friend who lived at the bottom of the hill when I was growing up. After my therapy, I started wondering about who else might have fallen victim to

Benny, and I wondered about Donny since he lived next door to him. I recalled now that Donny never wanted anything to do with Benny. I began thinking about the time Donny and I were playing catch in his back yard and I threw the baseball too high for him to catch and it landed in Benny's back yard. Donny wouldn't go get the ball and he told me to go get it. I went for the ball and when I returned Donny asked me to switch sides with him. At the time, I never gave it a second thought. Only lately did things like this start coming together. I would have liked to have talked to Donny and tell him what happened to me. If something similar had happened to him, maybe in some way we could have helped each other cope.

As I continued walking through the graveyard my thoughts went back to the good times I had in Hopewell Junction and all of my friends. I was hoping I would get the chance to see several of them on this trip. My mind was drifting when all of a sudden something caught my eye. It was the name on a headstone – Benny's headstone. I had heard several years ago that he had died but never dreamed of running into his grave. So here he was. So many emotions spiraled through me. I thought about how he urinated in front of me and how I tasted it when he shoved his penis in my mouth. Then the thought ran through my mind – "After what he did to me I should pee right here on his grave. That would show him." I looked around and no one was within sight. So I guess my ego was alive and well and ready to put in its two cents whenever the opportunity arose. I stood there for about five minutes thinking about it. "Who would blame me after what he did? Maybe it would make me feel better." Maybe it was that one action that could bring closure to this whole thing for me and give me a sense of retaliation. How tempting! But that was the thing. An action like that would say more about me than about him, and I knew that I had felt bad about myself long enough. Urinating on his grave would be putting more negative energy into a situation that I already had given too much of my time, thoughts, and emotions. It was time to let go and move on. That is what I had worked on in therapy and that is what I had been doing in my efforts to become more spiritually aware. So, I didn't do it; I just walked away and continued to look for my friend Donny's gravesite. I found him, paid my respects, had a talk with him, and left to go back to town to look up some more old friends who were still living in the area. Walking back out of the graveyard I felt so good about the fact that I was able to do the right thing at Benny's grave, and I felt really proud of myself knowing how far I had come in my healing process.

So, I can't say when or how it happened but over time I was able to really feel like I had forgiven Benny. I know it began that night when I pulled off of the road and realized what I had to do. And I know that feeling the unconditional love of God was also at work in the process. I am in no way making excuses for Benny or saying that what he did to me wasn't dreadfully wrong and painful. I'm just saying that I was able to release the negative thinking patterns associated with that incident. And forgiveness really had nothing to do with Benny, and everything to do with my own spiritual growth; wanting to clear anything that was blocking my ability to feel good about myself and to feel closer to God, and in doing so I have noticed that my inner spark is a little bit brighter.

EPILOGUE

I often have wondered why the incident in the woods, my motorcycle accident, my moments in Heaven and my return occurred in my life. I think most of us have an innate desire to believe that the major events that cross our lives do so for a larger reason or purpose. I guess I fall into that group. After I recovered from my accident I began thinking about these things a great deal. I knew I was going to be in severe pain for a long time and a great amount of pain for the rest of my life due to the extensive injuries I incurred. Wouldn't it have been easier and better for me to not have come back? So why DID I come back? What did I still need to complete?

While I was in the presence of the Light I thought of nothing related to the earth and I felt no pull or desire to come back – no thoughts about anything or anyone except how good it felt to be in the presence of that Light. I do believe in soul contracts so maybe that is why I am still on Earth. Maybe I have not reached the spiritual awareness I was meant to achieve in this lifetime or perhaps I need to help someone else fulfill theirs. However, I also believe in free will as one of God's greatest gifts to us. So it would seem that we do have a choice as to whether or not we complete our contracts. It still is quite complicated and I have many questions that remain unresolved. I would like to say that since my time in Heaven, I have become a perfect person and no longer have problems or issues or times when I get angry, or any of the other human emotions that occur when we let our egos guide our way, or at least succumb to them when we know we should be making better choices. But, I can't say that I have been able to do these things. I have been able to tap into the feeling I felt while in Heaven only as a memory. I have not felt that type of love since I returned to my physical body. But I do know that it is there, waiting for me. And that awareness had led me to make positive changes in my life. What I have accomplished with this knowledge is to forgive myself for what happened to me as a nine-year-old boy who was being sexually abused by an older boy, and I have learned to forgive him too. So maybe that was my unfinished business.

I have written about my experience in the woods for several reasons. For one, it is so much a part of my background and I know that many of the choices I have made in life have been a result of the fall-out of that incident. As trauma or abuse often does, this incident caused me to stop growing socially and emotionally. I advanced in age but lost the ability to mature in a normal manner. The impact it had on me was huge and I want to let others who have endured similar experiences know that they are not crazy. Trauma and abuse can change the way you think about yourself, others, and the world. I also wanted to let readers know that it is possible to forgive even those who have brought a very negative experience into your life, but it is by no means easy. I carried this burden of guilt, shame, low self-esteem, distrust of others, anger and many other emotions around for a long time. Then I realized that I was the one being damaged by these feelings – I was hurting only myself and I figured I had hurt long enough. As many have said, forgiving someone is really a gift we give ourselves. I thought it was equally as important for me to extend a hand of support to those who have been victimized by physical or sexual abuse as it was to share my message of Heaven. For me, learning to forgive and the love I felt at Heaven's door both were such healing forces in my life. If you have been abused, please know that there is help out there. Find a therapist or counselor you trust and ask them how they can help you. Each of us is different and the same type of therapy does not work for everyone, so make sure whatever you do sounds right for you.

My story is not as specific as many others who have had a Heavenly experience and spent time in another dimension. I did not receive any messages on what I was doing right or wrong, see loved ones who had died, or come back with special metaphysical skills, or answers to life's toughest questions. I did not see a tunnel or visual images of angels, God, Jesus, Buddha or other masters or teachers. But everyone's experiences are different. I believe that what I felt and learned in those moments were exactly what I needed in order to proceed with my spiritual growth. It has made a significant difference in my life and so I wanted to share it with you. It has become a mission for me to share it with as many people as possible through the words in this book and speaking engagements. If I had to explain the experience in one sentence, it would be *"love is by far the most powerful force existing."* If you have been unable to experience pure love in this lifetime, please know that you will experience it once you leave this earth. And, if you have been fortunate enough to find the love of your life while on this earthly journey, know that the love that awaits you once you transition to Spirit is at least one hundred to the hundredth degree as deep and pure and unconditional as the love you now feel. Know that our loving Creator thinks the world of you and wants you to know His love.

I will see you there.

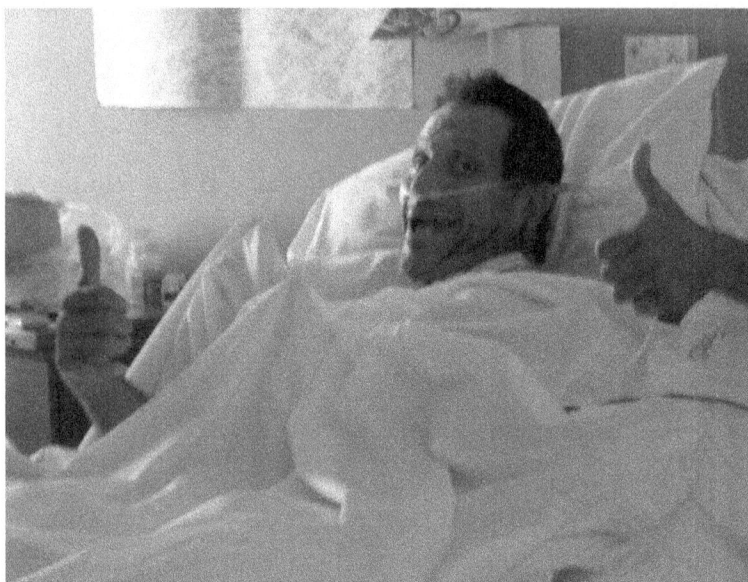

Just a few moments after I woke up

www.ingramcontent.com/pod-product-compliance
Lightning Source LLC
Chambersburg PA
CBHW030156070426
42447CB00031B/731